Old CASTLE DOUGLAS

by
Alastair Penman

Mr Dalling beside his saddlery caravan. He advertised that he would call at every farm in Dumfriesshire – 'Keep your repairs till we come. It will pay you'. His speciality was riding saddle repairs, and some of his wares, mainly plough-horse collars, are on display in front of his caravan. The Dalling family lived at Violet Grove in Castle Douglas.

First published in the United Kingdom, 1998,
by Stenlake Publishing
Telephone / Fax: 01290 551122

ISBN 1 84033 035 X

ACKNOWLEDGEMENTS

The author is very grateful to the following for their help in the research
and writing of this book: E.J. Cochrane, Jo Laurie, Jean C. Gibson,
Ian Devlin, George Livingston, Allan Phin, and George McCann.
A special thanks to Dr David Devereux, Curator of The Stewartry
Museum, Kirkcudbright, for all his help and encouragement.

The publishers would like to thank Robert Grieves for providing the
photograph that appears on the front cover. Thanks are also due to
Barry Smart and Andrew Low, who gave permission for the use of
postcards published by Adam Rae and John Low respectively.

The old boathouse at The Common, Carlingwark Loch – hard by what was once
a favourite place for local women to wash their blankets. This event was referred
to as the 'blanket fair' and took place during the days of spring cleaning. Huge
cauldrons were set up in the park, and the blankets were boiled and trampled in
wooden vats, before being rinsed, mangled and spread over dry-stane dykes to
dry. Not very far from here, on Fir Island, is the spot where it is reputed that
King Edward I of England had a blacksmith's forge built to shoe his troop's
cavalry horses, during his invasion of Galloway in 1300. Ancient horseshoes
have been recovered from the mud and, until 1875 when it was demolished, the
remains of a forge could apparently still be seen. Also called Dog Island by
locals, Fir Island is the last resting place of Prince, who was for twelve years
companion to Lady Abercromby of Birkenbog. He died in 1863 and the small
memorial and sculpture of Prince can still be seen.

INTRODUCTION

In 1765 the village of Carlingwark, formerly called Causewayend and named after the loch it was built beside, consisted of a few stone cottages and an ale-house. It was situated on the old road to Portpatrick hard by a Druidical sacrificial centre and trysting-place as ancient as time itself – the Three Thorns of Carlinwark.

The land on which the village stood had once been part of the estates of the Earls of Douglas – the infamous 'Black' Douglases. This land was originally bestowed upon them by Robert Bruce, but in 1455 all Douglas property was confiscated by King James II after the family rose in rebellion against the monarch. Following the fall of the Douglas's mighty fortress of Threave Castle their lands were taken into care, on the Crown's behalf, by the Maxwell family who acted as stewards. They eventually obtained the land rights for themselves and later sold these on to the Gordon family.

By the mid-eighteenth century the proprietor of the land was William Gordon of Culvennan, Sheriff Depute of Kirkcudbright, who recognised the potential of a vast strata of marl – a lime-based mineral – as a fertiliser. This substance was found in the mosses round Carlingwark Loch, and there was such a demand for it from local farmers that Sheriff Gordon started to have it dug out. In 1765 he built a canal from the loch to the River Dee so that the marl could be transported to farms along the banks of the river – including his own – from Kirkcudbright in the south to Dalry in the north. He improved the roads to make them more accessible to carts and waggons, and soon the whole area around the loch began to assume a new aspect. Labourers were brought in both to procure the marl and to improve communications. While digging out marl evidence was found of prehistoric occupation dating back to the Neolithic era and Bronze Age.

Gordon then proceeded to feu out parcels of land to his workers – at very agreeable prices – and as the village grew, so artisans, shop-keepers and the like were attracted there to settle. Ale-houses sprang up, service industries flourished and by 1789 the population of Carlingwark had increased to between 600 and 700 people. By 1792 the town bustled with flax-dressers and weavers, tanners, saddlers, cotton spinners, masons and carpenters.

Sheriff Gordon was one of those unfortunate enough to lose all of his savings in the collapse of a bank which had been based in Ayr – 'Bankers in Air' they have been wryly called. He was forced to recoup some of his losses by selling his marl works, loch and village of Carlingwark to William Douglas, a merchant-adventurer from Penningham, recently returned home from making his fortune in the Americas. The New Galloway moralist, Robert Heron, tells how he visited the town and, in 1793, found that:

. . . the number of its inhabitants was augmented, therefore, by incomers from Ireland, the Irish being like the Scotch, strongly disposed to emigrate to any country richer than their own. It became the favourite haunt, too, of wandering beggars; and many houses of entertainment for this class of guests were soon opened in it. Being advantageously situate for intercourse with both the sea-coasts and the inland country, it soon became likewise a seat of smugglers. It seemed to be rather the retreat of idleness, of want and of vice, than a scene of cheerful, thriving, virtuous industry.

However, William Douglas's vast personal fortune changed all this! A former privateer, Douglas was born in 1745 as the last embers of the Stuart dynasty were burning out. He made his money, rather dubiously, in the Americas, with more than one accusation of piracy and insurance fraud levelled against him. After making his fortune he opted to settle in his native Stewartry of Kirkcudbright and adopt the life of a country laird. He paid William Gordon the sum of £14,000 for Carlingwark village and loch and one of his first actions was to obtain, in December of 1791, a Burgh of Barony for his newly purchased town which he then proceeded to name Castle Douglas – after himself.

Douglas's personal motto was *Audax et Promptus* which means 'daring and ready'. With this outlook and both influential connections and a burning desire to 'improve' his new acquisition, Douglas became the superior and benefactor of the fledgling Burgh of Castle Douglas. Magistrates, elected by the feuars, governed it, and a courthouse was built to give form and dignity to their meetings. A prison and a school followed. Banks were opened and churches were founded until Douglas's Burgh – as it was referred to by Robert Burns – was equal to or better than others of its day.

The Georgian-style new town of Castle Douglas is a lasting monument to Sir William Douglas, who was elevated to the baronetcy he craved in 1801 and, when he died in 1809, buried in a magnificent tomb set beside the ancient parish church at Kelton. (It had been his wish to be buried in his burgh, in the new church in Queen Street, which is now the Parish Kirk, but the Church of Scotland were not impressed by the conditions laid down by Douglas. He had wanted an ornate marble tomb there, costing £1,000, for himself and his family, and a spire added to the kirk to give it importance.)

From Sir William's day his town has never looked back. By 1830 the population had increased to over 1,000 people, with the main industry classed as weaving. The Statistical Account of 1844 states that: '. . . this town, the suddenness of whose rise rivals the rapid growth of towns in America, has already attained an importance that, in most cases, is the growth of ages'. 154 years after this was written Castle Douglas is the thriving commercial capital of the Stewartry of Kirkcudbright. It can truly be said to hold to its motto of 'Forward' – the motto of Sir William Douglas – and let us hope that it will continue to go forward for all time.

On the night of 27 February 1934 the former town hall and clock tower burnt down. The premises below the clock tower, comprising two shops with rooms leased to Castle Douglas Billiard Club on the first floor, were completely gutted and the adjoining properties of Mr Burnett's hairdresser's shop and the Conservative Association Clubrooms were seriously damaged. The flames spread with great rapidity and, in an incredibly short space of time, the top portion of the building was ablaze. The fire was started, apparently, by a smouldering oak beam which had been burning slowly for a long time. On the night of the fire a wind had got up, the draft causing the beam to catch fire. This photograph, by the late James Gair, was taken a few hours after the calamity while the photographer was supported on a pulley outside one of the windows of the Commercial Hotel opposite. The current clock tower (right) was built in 1935 and is the third to stand on this site at the Cross.

Looking east up King Street from Rowena Place. The houses on the left in the middle distance have now been demolished to make way for a petrol station. In 1867 Castle Douglas was described as looking more like an overgrown village than a town. This part, the bottom of the town, was known as 'Wee Dublin', so named after its predominantly Irish immigrant population. Many of the houses were thatched, while in the upper portion of King Street nearly all of the properties were of one storey.

King Street, with the fire station and Brown's garage on the left. The Brown family, wheelwrights and carpenters, moved from Tinwald to the Castle Douglas area in the mid 1700s, and in 1832 the firm of James Brown was founded, building gigs, carts and broughams to customers' specifications. With the advent of the motor car, the business developed into coachbuilding (building bodies on to vehicle chassis), as well as undertaking general mechanical and body repairs.

KING STREET, CASTLE DOUGLAS

A more modern-looking Brown's Garage with the entrance to the firm's coachworks opposite. Brown's once had the contract for the maintenance of the stage-coaches which passed through Castle Douglas from Stranraer to London. The firm were also agents for the Essex Terraplane, a small car that was popular between the wars, and built van bodies onto Albion chassis for local businesses that required travelling shops to go round the farms and villages. The business still continues in the family and is now run by a fifth generation Brown.

The Cross was a popular meeting place in the town and the place where royal proclamations and other important items of news were publicly read out by the provost. It was to this 'centre', on Saturday nights, that the artisan and labourer, clean shaven and in holiday dress, gravitated after the labours of the week, to gossip and discuss the town's affairs, as well as those of the nation. It was the great 'mental victualling place' of the burgh, and as Malcolm Harper, an old resident, naively remarked, where 'monie a starving intellect got nourishment'. The arrival of the mail coach at the Douglas Arms, was also, in those days of scarce news, a signal for the collecting of groups of gossipers and crowds of onlookers on the look out for 'the latest news' from the city. The large premises next to the town clock occupies the space where the exit from the Douglas Arms Stables once was.

A. Rae, C.D.

*Douglas Arms Hotel,
King Street, Castle Douglas
Sept. 20/1904*

In early stage-coaching and posting days, Castle Douglas was situated on the main road to Portpatrick where the steamers to Ireland sailed from. Sir William Douglas, the town's founder, had been quick to see the advantages of its situation on the route leading to the shortest sea-crossing between Britain and Ireland. Thus the town became an important halting station. One early recollection was of the animation caused by the arrival, at the Douglas Arms, to the accompaniment of the blowing of a bugle, of the coach carrying Her Majesty's Royal Mail. The 'scarlet uniformed functionaries' assumed an air of importance among the ostlers, stable-boys and hangers-on at the coaching inn. Note Sir William Douglas's personal coat-of-arms above the hotel sign. He never in fact owned this establishment, and it is claimed that the Douglas Arms was a posting house, just outside the village of Carlingwark, long before Douglas ever came on the scene. The double-fronted shop on the left was where Mr McMeeken carried on his grocery business. It is now the cocktail bar of the present hotel.

KING STREET,
CASTLE DOUGLAS.

St George's Church was built in 1863 as a Free Church and eventually amalgamated with the Trinity Church in Abercromby Road and St Ringan's Church in Queen Street. St George's owed its existence to the Disruption of 1843 when many ministers and their flocks left the established Kirk of Scotland on matters which largely concerned the patronage system of appointing the clergy. After its amalgamation with St Ringan's Church in Queen Street in 1923, Mr Dalling (of the saddlery caravan) opened an antique shop in it and thenceforth the building was called 'Dalling's Kirk'. The building was subsequently demolished and a modern furniture store built on the site. The shop to the left of the cart in the foreground was a car showroom owned by A.C. Penman Ltd., who had to run vehicles in over the pavement as there was no accessible back entrance. They were succeeded by Messrs Napiers and then by Corson the Bakers who still occupy the site today. Corson's are the oldest private bakery firm in The Stewartry, started in the 1870s by a Miss Clark who, when she died in the 1920s, left the business to her niece Mrs Corson. The present owner is Mrs Corson's grandson.

KING STREET, CASTLE DOUGLAS

Looking up King Street. When the era of the motor car dawned, the Douglas Arms (left foreground), formerly a coaching house, made the transition from horsepower to internal combustion power and immediately opened a petrol filling station and garage beside the hotel. The car is parked next to its petrol pump.

King Street, Castle Douglas.

Looking towards the Cross with the petrol pumps of Payne's Garage (owned by the Douglas Arms) on the right. On the left are James Gordon the Stationers, Barr's the Chemist, and a dairy. Beyond, at the Cross, are the buildings of Oliver & McLean, Italian Warehousemen and above them the Commercial Hotel, which was originally built as a private house in 1820. The warehouse is now a Chinese restaurant, the hotel an Indian one.

On the right is the entrance to Thomas Corrie's Morris House. Beyond is the Douglas Arms Hotel and the most recent of the three town clocks to have been built on the site. Judging by the cars this photograph was taken after the Second World War.

The second of three town clocks, built in 1893, features in this photograph. The shop on the left is Kirk The Saddler, still in business under the management of the Kirk family. The Douglas Arms Hotel, founded over 200 years ago, held the reputation of being the most commodious and comfortable hotel in the county. It was selected as fitting quarters for Her Majesty's (Queen Victoria) Mail. The proprietrix at one time was a Mrs Douglas who, in the rising days of the burgh, was a popular and respected landlady. The name of Douglas was so much associated with the place that it was not uncommon for Sir William Douglas, staying in the hotel while his castle was being built near Gelston Raw, to receive his mail addressed to Sir William Douglas, of Douglas Castle, care of Mrs Douglas, Douglas Arms, Castle Douglas.

King Street, with the premises of R.C. Brown's, Ironmongers, on the left. Mr Brown used to serve his customers wearing a black hat, Churchill-style wing collar and gold watch-chain across his waistcoat. Also immaculately dressed was his sister and assistant, Miss Bessie Brown, who left a considerable sum of money to the town in the form of the Brown Bequest when she died in the 1940s. It is still used to supply bags of coal to the senior citizens of the burgh every Christmas – on application. The building on the right has been partially demolished to make way for an entry leading to private housing.

Looking west down King Street. The building on the right is now the post office; the one on the left is McCrindle's the Chemists. It was formerly a branch of Boots. A modern store now stands on the site of St George's Church.

KING STREET, CASTLE DOUGLAS.   83599. J.V.

The Crown Hotel was a licensed rest-house and posting house in coaching days. The Wallet family, proprietors when this picture was taken, were also carriers as well as owners of Wallet's Marts. One can imagine the scene as if it were yesterday: the processions of Wallet's carts slowly passing down the street, guarded by a fierce-looking brindled bull-dog. The vehicles were drawn by powerful steady-going horses, led by stoutly built weather-beaten drivers, in moleskin-sleeved waistcoats with plush fronts and ivory buttons as large as half-crown pieces. The entry just beyond the hotel led to the Crown Garage, now owned and run by the Haugh family.

Looking east up Queen Street. The white building third on the left was William Innes's brewery. It eventually made way for Billy Slater's picture house, affectionately known as 'Billie's' to generations of schoolchildren. On a wet day sensible people took an umbrella with them as the tin roof leaked copiously, although the best films were always shown there. It was succeeded by the King's Arms Hotel garage and is now a yard used for car parking. The basement of the cottage next to the brewery was a bottle store and the two buildings were joined by an underground passage which was excavated in the late 1960s and found to be full of old bottles. Brewing was a popular local business. Nearly all of the local grocers and chemists produced brews in their own distinctive bottles – now collector's items.

A view looking west on Queen Street. The large building on the right is Chapel Place, once a doctor's surgery, and home of former Provost Dr T.M. Donald, a veteran of the Monte Carlo Rally. The trees on the left are outside St Ringan's Church, formerly the Cameronian Kirk and now Castle Douglas Parish Church. This was the site that Sir William Douglas chose for his last resting-place, although the Presbyterian Kirk Elders, always douce men, were not impressed by his plans for an ornate marble tomb, and despite his importance in life Douglas's body had to lie elsewhere. The Cameronian Kirk, a throwback to the days of the Covenanters, was noted for its austerity and length of services. To qualify to take communion worshippers had to present themselves on a Thursday to be tested on their knowledge of things spiritual. If they passed this they were presented with a token, which was their admission to the Communion table on the Sabbath.

QUEEN STREET, CASTLE DOUGLAS.

Looking west down Queen Street. William Douglas's town was planned with the streets laid out on a grid plan, and the early part of the town comprises blocks of parallel streets.

Departure of G.Coy. 5th K.O.S.B.

John Low,
Castle-Douglas.

The departure of G Coy 5th Battalion of the King's Own Scottish Borderers for war on 7 August 1914, three days after the declaration of hostilities. 29 out of the 101 officers and other ranks who paraded that morning never returned.

RAILWAY STATION, CASTLE DOUGLAS 34.

Castle Douglas station, now the site of a garage and motor showroom, was once famous for the beauty of its prize-winning gardens. The station saw much activity in the days of the railway from Dumfries to Stranraer. In 1859 the local Castle Douglas and Dumfries Railway Company opened a line between the two towns. Half of the cost was met by the Glasgow and South Western Railway Company and the other half was raised by public subscription. The Portpatrick Railway was opened in 1861 and four years later, in 1865, amalgamated with the G&SWR. 100 years later Dr Beeching announced the closure of this 'Paddy Line'.

Great festivities marked the opening of the new railway on 7 November 1859, with a large gathering at the new station to welcome the first regular train into Galloway. The town council, led by Provost Nicholson, walked up King Street in a body preceded by a handsome new flag, while the Gatehouse of Fleet Band enlivened the proceedings. In the evening a bonfire was lit on 'Myre's Mount', the eminence on the Market Hill behind the present tourist information centre, where a display of fireworks was witnessed by most of the burgh's citizenry.

Looking south along St Andrew Street. On the left is the 'new' town hall, built in 1862. It was described as being able to hold 500 to 600 people, although modern regulations now preclude a gathering of this size. During the last century it was the meeting-place of the commissioners of supply, courts, council and police commission. The Mechanic's Institute had a reading room (described as 'commodious') and an excellent library in the same building. Immediately adjacent was the Union Bank of Scotland, and across the road the post office, an insignificant-looking building but one of the most important in the South of Scotland as a despatching office. There were two deliveries in the town daily, and two collections from the pillar box near the Free Kirk (St George's) in King Street. The old Town House was situated at the foot of the town clock steeple. It was built by Sir William Douglas in 1790, burned down in 1892, and was replaced by shops and rooms for hire, the revenue from which went into the town's 'Common Good Fund', which still exists to-day.

ST, ANDREWS STREET, CASTLE DOUGLAS,

The Palace Cinema, on the left, was built by Harold Dobie. It didn't only show films, and many artistes visited the town; the Glasgow Orpheus Choir were frequent performers there. The building was owned and run by a consortium of local businessmen – Castle Douglas Theatres Ltd. – but the guiding light was Harold Dobie. He was a man of great vision and foresight and embarked on a project to bring the electric cinema to Castle Douglas. He started off at the Ashley Hall, now the Masonic Lodge, and then built The Palace. Harold's widow, Mary ('Ma' Dobie), ran the cinema for many years after his death, and often spoke of Harold's many inventions and his fascination with electricity and bicycles.

An open-air animal market was originally held on this piece of common land, which was surrounded by a dry-stane dyke for the purpose. The main fair, when horses from all over the country were brought to be bought and sold, was held in June. In 1856 Thomas Wallet sold eight sheep and a few Galloway cattle on this spot and so, unwittingly, began the business of cattle-dealing which brought the greatest prosperity to the town. The land was subsequently used by customers of the Wallet brothers nearby market. The main area is now a car park, and there are swings and roundabouts at the end nearest the war memorial. Unusually, in this day and age, it is still possible to park your car here, free of charge, for as long as you want.

In 1860, with the demise of the Keltonhill Fair, which had been held annually at the nearby village of Rhonehouse for as long as could be remembered, the way was open for a new venue to cater for the huge numbers of people who gathered to attend the annual festivity. Wallet's Marts filled this gap and following its establishment expanded continually over the next forty years, until by the early years of the twentieth century it was a rambling site comprising a wide assortment of buildings covering over seven acres of ground. The byres and pens of the mart could accommodate about 2,000 cattle and 30,000 sheep. It was instantly recognisable by its main ring, housed inside the distinctive building shown here.

Ewen's the Jewellers in King Street was established by J.S. Ewen in the late nineteenth century. Mr Ewen was not only a jeweller, but also an ophthalmic optician and watchmaker. He was followed by his son, also J.S., and he in turn by his son. At one time, a cairngorm, described as one of the largest and finest in the country, was displayed in a glass case inside the shop. The tall gentleman in the middle of the group is Mr Ewen, the founder of the business. Note that this jeweller, unusually, but in common with several others in the area, was a purveyor of fishing tackle too.

Builders of landaus, barouches, Victorias, broughams and stage-coaches, Penman's Garage in Cotton Street had a reputation for craftsmanship. With the advent of the motor car they moved into building vehicle bodies for Albion Motors in 1902. In 1928 A.C. Penman Ltd. was formed consolidating the Penman businesses in Castle Douglas, Dalbeattie, Moffat, Ayr and Kirkcudbright. The Penman family originally came from Carronbridge where they had been blacksmiths and wheelwrights to the Duke of Buccleuch. Amongst other vehicles they built mail-coaches which were packed in giant wooden crates (cost £8 7s 4d each) and taken south on railway goods waggons. The motor cars in the picture are both Albions. SM 261 was a 16 horsepower Albion Brougham, painted green and registered on 20 September 1907 by Robert McGregor of New Cumnock. The other vehicle is probably another of the 16 horsepower models built by Penman's in Castle Douglas. Their workshops are now Corson's Bakers yard.

E Coy of the Volunteer Battalion of the Royal Scots Fusiliers at Caigton Camp. The occasion of the breakdown of this traction engine, in 1909, was deemed important enough to be the subject matter on a postcard of the time. 200 years ago the old name of the farm where the camp was held was Craigton and now it is once again called by that name.

CAIGTON CAMP

The first camp of the newly formed 5th (Dumfries & Galloway) Battalion of the King's Own Scottish Borderers, held at Caigton (now Craigton) Farm in July 1908. Caigton continued in use as a Territorial Army rifle range until the 1960s and the author well remembers many happy hours spent there in good company.

G Coy. 5th Battalion King's Own Scottish Borderers photographed outside the Territorial Army drill hall (now the town swimming pool) three days after the declaration of war in 1914. In the middle of the third row is Captain Ernest Switzer Forde, a local GP and provost of the burgh of Castle Douglas from 1925 to 1938. A veteran of the Egypt (1888) and Boer Wars (1899-1902), he served as a medical officer in the Dardanelles and France and was wounded at Cape Hellas. Seated on his left is Lt. Salmond, later the headmaster of Creetown School, who was invalided home from Gallipoli. The Battalion served with great distinction in the Gallipoli campaign of 1915 but bore very heavy casualties; out of 50 officers and 1082 men, the 1/5th Battalion lost 30 officers and 760 men in this disastrous campaign. They went on to fight in Egypt, Gaza and the Western Front. The most decorated Castle Douglas soldier was Pte. J.J. O'Haire who won the Military Medal and both the French Medaille Militaire and Croix de Guerre with Palms for continuous gallantry and devotion to duty at Beugneux. The French decorations were presented on the field. Pte. O'Haire was killed in action in 1918.

The former High School in Cotton Street was built by the Kelton School Board and designated a 'B' school to distinguish it from the parish school in Academy Street, which continued as an 'A' school. Mr Cowper, who had formerly been the headmaster of 'Cowper's Schule' a few metres down the street, and educator of such local worthies as S.R. Crockett and W.S. McGeorge, took charge of it until 1874. It remained the high school until its successor was built off Dunmuir Road in 1958. The handsome red sandstone building is now the local community centre. Sir William Douglas's hopes for a thriving industrial community were centred on Cotton Street. But it was only to be a hive of industry for a few years, and by the time that this school was built the majority of buildings were private houses rather than mills.

Looking westwards (East) up Cotton Street. On the left is the church of St John the Evangelist, built in 1867 to serve the increasing Roman Catholic population immigrating from Ireland to build roads, canals and railways. Prior to that date, on this site, stood a little cottage occupied by Andrew Graham, a weaver after whose trade the street was named. Just beyond the telephone pole on the left is the cottage where the novelist S.R. Crockett lived. In *Raiderland* he described the Castle Douglas people as 'the kindliest-hearted folk in the world'. The building on the right was built as a linen mill and subsequently became a glove factory, then a garage. It is now sheltered housing. Just behind the houses on the left is The Cockhill, described in 1907 as being a little green knoll in a locality so secluded that the 'sporting gentry' of the town resorted there with their birds to engage in the barbarous sport of cock-fighting, as a safe retreat from the ever watchful eye of Willie Graham, the Burgh Officer. Much of it has now been built upon.

Crossmichael Road, Castle-Douglas

Abercromby Road, affectionately known locally as the Crossmichael Road – because it led to Crossmichael village – was where the local merchants built their grander houses in the nineteenth century. A feature of this road was the diversity of ironwork in the railings, testifying to the skill of the local blacksmiths. The chimneys, too, vary from house to house, and on some houses there is sandstone carving on a modest scale. The Relief Chapel, now the site of a private garden, stood on the right behind the wall. The land on the left of the road was feued out by the Abercromby family, thus the name of the road, but the land on the right was owned by local farmers and the feu duties went to them. The story goes that the Abercrombys, on occasion, asked only for one white rose as their feu duty.

Curling on Carlingwark Loch, Castle-Douglas.

Castle Douglas was well known as the home of the Queenshill Cup, a curling trophy famous throughout the south-west. Donated in 1864 by wealthy inventor Robert Beaumont Neilson, who, in 1828, had developed the hot blast system of smelting iron ore, the cup was one of the most prestigious trophies in local curling contests. It was named after Neilson's Stewartry home at Ringford. A rule stipulated that the trophy had to be played for on Carlingwark Loch, which only froze over eight times in the first 30 years of the competition. The trophy has not been played for at all in the last fourteen years as there has been little or no ice. When the statutory five inches of ice was in place on the loch, the word went out that 'The Queenshill' was on! Farms were left to look after themselves, businesses closed, and many professional gentlemen found that they needed to take a very hurried holiday. All congregated at Carlingwark Loch where the rinks were opened and the 'roaring game' commenced. The author well remembers playing truant from school to ferry the sets of curling stones to and from the rinks, while their owners concentrated on carefully carrying their bottles of 'warming refreshment'. A well paid job for many a local schoolboy!

Threave Terrace, Castle Douglas.

Bottom and Top Threave Terrace are said by many to have the best view in the burgh. Top Threave Terrace was built along the line of the original Portpatrick coach road, and the Carlingwark Inn, where Robert Burns once stayed, was situated approximately where the house at the top left now stands. Of his stay in the town he wrote to an Edinburgh friend, Mrs Agnes McLehose (Clarinda) on 25 June 1794: 'Here am I set a solitary hermit, in a solitary room, of a solitary inn, with a solitary bottle of wine by me'. Another letter, written to his patroness Mrs Dunlop of Dunlop, also from Carlingwark Inn, reads: 'Castle Douglas, here in a solitary inn, in a solitary village, am I set by myself, to amuse my brooding fancy as I may.' There was an ancient trysting-place at this spot, and it is recorded how two feuding local landowners from Urr, Maxwell of Newark and McNaight, the laird of Kilquhanity, met here one night in April 1612. McNaight was slain by two of Maxwell's kinsmen 'in the house of one John Hutton'. No-one was ever brought to trial for the murder.

The elephant's ablutions, which were carried out in Carlingwark Loch, were apparently a common sight when the circus visited Castle Douglas before the First World War. The washing place got the name of the 'Elephant Hole' and the name survived long after the circus had disappeared for good. According to local folklore, a 'toun' was drowned beneath the water near this spot. There had previously been two chapels, one on each of two islands, and it was said that during very dry seasons – that of 1825 being referred to in particular – the roofs of the sunken chapels were seen in the loch. On stormy nights residents on Carlingwark Hill reported hearing the chimes of ghostly bells tolling underwater, presumably the sound of the long drowned church bells ringing out as a reminder of their existence in another time. Now a site of special scientific interest, the loch is home to many birds today. In winter the geese and ducks come and in the summer it is a prolific breeding area for many rare species. Coots, moorhens and mallard all abound and 3% of all the mute swans in Scotland live permanently on Carlingwark Loch.

The circus was an ever popular attraction, especially between the wars when there was not much local entertainment. On one visit an elephant died and, because of its size, had to be taken out of town to be buried. The burial place is still a closely guarded secret. On an eminence by the side of Carlingwark Loch there used to be a grove of ancient hawthorn trees called The Three Thorns of Carlinwark. According to local tradition, three singularly powerful and dangerous spirits, who could resurrect corpses for their own unholy purposes, used to meet at the trees. Strange Celtic rites and sacrifices would have taken place within sight of the quiet waters of the Loch, when sacrificial victims (individuals who were greatly honoured and pampered in their last days) would be bound with cords and virtually ripped to death by the cult's high priest – the Druid. He would carefully scrutinise the death-throes of the victim for omens. A similar examination of the late departed's entrails was believed to aid the Druid in divining the future. Finally the head of the corpse would be severed then ritually bound in a cord and the gory trophy treated with great respect for ever more.

CHILDRENS PLAYGROUND, CASTLE DOUGLAS

For a long time Lochside Park was a play area for local children. After regionalisation it was let out as stances for tents and caravans, and the play area moved off to one side where it still is today. Here, too, the many circuses and amusement fairs which visited the burgh pitched their tents and stalls. 'The Common' as this park was originally called, was given to the town by Sir William Douglas and included a walled- or fenced-in area where any burgher could graze their livestock. Many families were grateful for the use of a space to graze a goat, cow or a few sheep in order to supplement their often meagre rations.

BOWLING GREEN, CASTLE DOUGLAS.

6208

The land occupied by the bowling green was gifted to the town by Sir William Douglas in the early nineteenth century. At one time there was a quoiting green adjacent to it, but that has now been built upon.

The King George V Coronation procession on 22 June 1911, coming down the 'Slaughterhouse Brae' at the east end of Cotton Street. The local Boys' Brigade are to the fore, followed by the town band then the Town Council, led by Provost Adam Rae, a newsagent. The Jubilee Fountain is visible in the background at the top of the hill.

This procession, making its way up King Street, may well have been organised to mark the accession to the throne of King Edward VII in 1902. The large sandstone building in the centre of the photograph is the Clydesdale Bank, built in 1890. It supplanted one-storeyed cottages on the site. The gap in the street where the derrick stands is now occupied by the Imperial Hotel. Parades and processions were a way of life amongst a people who had a fierce and unquestioning national pride and loyalty to the throne, as the population of Great Britain had prior to the international calamity of the 1914-18 War.

Crowds of onlookers gathered to see a collapsed hot air balloon. The occasion was a sports day in July 1906, held on what is now the golf coarse. The large white building back right was St Andrew's Station, which faced on to Abercromby Road. Built in 1864, it only remained in use for some three years and after closing in 1867 was turned into private housing. Passengers had to be put down at this point and conveyed to the station at the top of the town by Mr Payne's carriage to catch their connections. This was because the Board of Trade deemed the last 600 yards of railway line to be unsafe, and not fit to be traversed by passenger trains. Luckily goods traffic was not included in this ban. The spire to the left of the station is that of Trinity Church. It was amalgamated with St George's in King Street, and St Ringan's in Queen Street, and ended up being the church hall for St Ringan's. It was then sold and used as a carpenter's store for a time before being converted into flats.

The aftermath of the fire of 24 May 1904 in King Street, which gutted shops and the houses above them. Mr Grierson, a local builder, repaired and rebuilt the property and proceeded to advertise the houses and shops for rent. They were then customised to suit the requirements of their new occupiers. One was taken by Mr Livingston, a tailor, whose great-grandson is still in business there. Beyond the burnt shops is Walker's the chemist and below that is Lawson's. Mr Walker's lemonade is still well remembered by the logo of a walking man on the – now very collectible – bottles.

The Buchan,
Castle Douglas.

The coach road to Portpatrick went right past the front doors of these little cottages at the Buchan. Situated only feet within the burgh boundary, this is oldest part of Castle Douglas. It is the place described in traditional tales as the site of the smithy owned and run by Brawny McKim and his seven sons. The forge was thought to have been in the farthest away house. In 1455, when James II was besieging the mighty castle of Threave, he brought artillery with him from Stirling. None of it was capable of breaching the strong defences of the nearby stronghold of the 'Black Douglases' and he commissioned McKim to build him a monster 'bombard' or cannon with which to batter down the walls of the castle. Apparently each burgher of Kirkcudbright town was made to contribute one 'gaud' or bar of iron towards the construction of this monster and when it was finished it was dragged on a waggon to Glenlochar Hill and there dug into the ground, set at an elevation of 45 degrees, and fired at Threave castle. Only three shots were launched! After the third, said to have taken off the hand of the 'Fair Maid of Galloway' as she sat at table sipping from a glass of wine – 'the same hand that had been given in wedlock to two brothers' – the castle surrendered and King James II rewarded the McKims with money and lands.

46

The lily blooms in Carlingwark, the daisy by the Dee,
The wild rose scents the Lovers' Walk and fair Ernespie lea;
But this bit heather that I send has charms to you mair dear,
Near Mary o' the Moss's cot it grew for mony a year.—*G. G. B. Sproat.*

Mary O'The Moss's Cottage, Castle Douglas.

Mary o' the Moss's cottage on the lands of Torrs Farm, just outside the burgh boundary. Mary worked at the Oakwell Woollen Mills and lived on Torrs Moss, an area of land between the two roads leading south out of the town. This area was under water in prehistoric times, part of the ancient Carlingwark Loch system. The cottage was beside an ancient pathway, still in use today, and may have originally been built as a shelter for a family whose prime duty would have been to keep an eye on the cows and sheep grazing there lest they wander into the bog. There is a painting of the interior of the cottage, by Malcolm Harper, in the Stewartry Museum Collection, showing it with a cobbled floor and a large water-butt beside an open fireplace. It is still just possible to discern the site of the cottage from the remnants of its garden, where berry and currant bushes still grow alongside a plum tree.

The original name of Ernespie House was *Ard-en-espic* (the mound or hill of the Bishop), after the eminence in front of the house which has now been reclaimed for agricultural use. Situated on the Castle Douglas burgh boundary, this property originally belonged to the Gordons of Lochinvar, having been granted to them on 21 June 1621. The present mansion was built by Peter Lawrie, who is listed as the owner in the valuation roll of 1799. His daughter, Anne, married John McKie MP of Bargally, in Minnigaff, in 1817. She and her husband inherited the estate and it passed to his their son, also called John, who was MP for the Stewartry of Kirkcudbright from the 1850s until his sudden death, at Ernespie, in 1867. Politics seem to have run in the McKie's (or Mackies) blood. There was a James McKie MP sitting in Parliament in 1874, and another John MacKie, the Liberal MP for Galloway from 1929 to 1958 claimed to be the sixth member of his family to have represented the province in Parliament. He, incidentally, was probably the last MP to refuse to accept a salary. This picture shows the front door of the house with the owner, Mrs Lawrence, sitting in her personal carriage.